MAR 1998

W9-DEX-878

YOUR PET TROPICAL FISH

A TRUE BOOK

by

Elaine Landau

Children's Press®
A Division of Grolier Publishing

New York London Hong Kong Sydney
Danbury, Connecticut

Reading Consultant
Linda Cornwell
Learning Resource Consultant
Indiana Department
of Education

Author's Dedication:
For Jerry, Bianca,
and Abraham

A school of
guppies

Library of Congress Cataloging-in-Publication Data

Landau, Elaine.
    Your pet tropical fish / by Elaine Landau.
        p.   cm. — (A True book)
    Includes bibliographical references and index.
    Summary: Discusses many kinds of tropical fish and explains the basics
    of fish care.
    ISBN 0–516–20386–X (lib. bdg.)   0-516-26278-5 (pbk.)
    1. Tropical fish—Juvenile literature. 2. Aquariums—Juvenile Literature.
    [1. Tropical fish. 2. Aquarium fishes 3. Aquariums 4. Fishes. 5. Pets.] I.
    Title. II. Series.
SF457.25.L35 1997
639. 34—dc21   97–17378
                                                                                    CIP
                                                                                    AC

Contents

You can make your aquarium a beautiful underwater world.

Keeping Tropical Fish

Picture a beautiful underwater world. Brilliantly colored fish glide past plants, castle ruins, and sunken treasure chests. A tiny fish darts out from behind a blue rock. It could be a tropical paradise—or it could be your very own aquarium.

Tropical fish are great pets. First, you don't need a lot of money to get started. Many tropical fish do not cost very much. And fish are smaller than most pets, so you can create an aquarium to fit your room.

Also, fish do not have to be walked. And your neighbors will never complain that your pets are being too noisy.

Creating a tropical fish aquarium takes some planning, and keeping one takes some work. But you will soon find that the results are worth the effort.

Tropical fish come in all sizes, from big to very small.

Choosing Your Fish

Tropical fish are sold in most pet shops. There are hundreds of kinds to choose from. The types most commonly available are usually hardy and colorful. These fish are naturally found in tropical waters. But the ones you buy at pet shops are usually bred in captivity.

You can find
tropical fish at
most pet shops.

If this is your first aquarium, start with only a few fish. All the fish described in this chapter are good for beginners. They require similar living conditions and can survive in a tank together.

Swordtail fish are a good choice for home aquariums. They are brightly colored, and the males have long tails that look like swords.

The harlequin rasbora is another popular fish. This

Swordtails dart in different directions.

small, brightly colored fish comes originally from east Asia. Although they look delicate, harlequins are known to resist disease and live a long time. Harlequins are also very peaceful.

A harlequin rasbora

These fish are called zebra danios because of their stripes.

The danio is another Asian fish. The small, slender danio always seems to be moving. The zebra danio has rows of tiny black specks forming dark stripes on its body.

A corydoras is
commonly known
as a catfish.

The corydoras is a small catfish. These hardy creatures are called catfish because they have whiskers near their mouths. Corydoras also have hard, bony plates or scales covering their bodies. Cory cats, as they are sometimes called, swim along the bottom of the tank in search of food.

The pearl gourami is a peaceful, delicate-looking fish with a lovely color pattern of

A pearl gourami

white, black, and purple. At mating time, the stomach area of the male pearl gourami turns bright orange.

There are many other fish you may want to add to your aquarium. Ask the manager of your pet store for suggestions. Just be sure that all the fish you choose need similar living conditions and can get along together in a tank.

A Rainbow of Fish

The spectacular colors of tropical fish make them fascinating to watch. Covered with brilliant blues, vibrant yellows, and bright oranges, some fish almost seem to glow.

Have fun adding
new, colorful fish to
your aquarium as it grows.

Basic Supplies

Before bringing home your tropical fish, you will need some basic supplies. These are a few of the more important items.

Buy the largest tank you can afford and have space for. After all, your pet fish won't be going out for a walk. The

Aquariums range from simple glass tanks (below) to elaborate and expensive setups (left).

tank will be their entire world. You'll find fish tanks in different sizes and shapes at your pet store. The store manager

Your local pet store can help you select the right tank and supplies for you fish.

can help you figure out how many fish can live in the tank you choose.

The water you put in your fish tank must be conditioned before being used. Figure out how much tap water you need, and let it stand for about two weeks before putting it in the fish tank. This gets rid of gases in the water that could be harmful to your fish. You can also buy products at your pet store to remove chlorine from the water.

Both the fish and the plants in an aquarium need light to thrive. Pet stores sell a special fluorescent light tube that fits into a cover placed on top of the tank.

Aquarium fish and plants also need oxygen. Make sure there is enough oxygen in your aquarium by installing an air pump. The pump produces a stream of air bubbles, adding oxygen to the water.

A filter helps keep the water clean. There are many different types of filters. Some internal ones fit inside the tank. External filters are usually

PENN PLAX *clear·free II*

This water filter fits inside your aquarium.

placed next to the aquarium or fastened to the outside of the tank. Remember to clean your aquarium filter regularly. This removes the dirt trapped in it.

Tropical fish need their water to be a certain temperature. You will need a water heater to make sure your aquarium stays at the proper temperature. Most heaters attach to the rim of the fish tank with a tube that hangs in

This heater will keep the water in your fish tank at the proper temperature for your fish.

the water. You will also need a thermometer that measures water temperature. Check it regularly to make sure that your heater is working properly.

An Underwater Wonderland

In addition to the basic supplies, you'll enjoy making your aquarium a beautiful and special place. River sand and gravel are sold in many colors at pet stores. Use them to cover the bottom of the tank.

Then you can add stones (only clean ones from a pet store), plants, castle ruins, tiny divers, and other miniature objects.

These "extras" do more than just improve how the tank looks. They provide private areas for the more timid fish. They also help divide the tank, allowing the fish to stake out their own territory.

Maintaining Your Aquarium

Your fish need a healthy living environment. Each week, replace about a quarter of your tank's water with conditioned water. Do this gradually to avoid a sudden temperature change. You will also

have to rid the tank of small impurities not caught by the filter. You can buy kits to test

You will need a net
for removing fish
from your aquarium.

the water for impurities that may harm your fish.

Dead plant matter must be removed from the tank. And algae buildup must be scraped off the aquarium's inner glass from time to time. Occasionally, you may need to transfer some fish to a temporary tank while maintaining your aquarium. You'll need a small net for removing your fish.

Feeding

Make sure your fish get a balanced diet. Pets stores sell fish foods containing the vitamins and minerals tropical fish need. These come in several different forms including powders, flakes, and pellets. You can enhance your fishes' diet by adding some live

Fish food can come in several forms, including flakes (left) and pellets (below).

You can add variety to your fishes' diet by feeding them live food such as tubifex worms (top) and brine shrimp (left).

food. Tubifex worms and brine shrimp are excellent choices and are also available in pet stores.

Watch your fish at feeding time to see how much they eat. Once you know the actual amount of food your fish need, be careful not to overfeed them. Too much food can harm your fish. And leftover food in the tank breaks down and pollutes the water in the aquarium.

A Sixth Sense

Do you know why fish never swim into the walls of their aquarium? Fish avoid crashes using a sense organ that humans do not have. It is called the lateral line, and it runs along the side of the fish from the eye to the tail. You can see the thin lateral line on some fish.

The arrow is pointing the the lateral line on this fish. Can you spot it on the sides of these other fish?

The lateral line gives the fish a sense between hearing and touch. As a fish swims past an object in the water, or as an object moves near the fish, disturbances are created in the water. The lateral line detects these disturbances and warns the fish of the nearby object.

You and Your Fish

Keeping tropical fish has become an extremely popular hobby. But it's not a new pastime. In ancient times, people in Rome and China kept aquariums. Sometimes fish were kept for enjoyment. Other times, they were stored in the tank only

Tropical fish are fascinating to watch as they explore their underwater environment.

Keeping an aquarium takes some work, but it's worth it.

until they were cooked and eaten.

Having an aquarium is both fun and educational. You will learn about many different fish and what they need to survive. You'll need to set aside some time each week to care for your fish, but you'll be rewarded by watching these colorful creatures explore their underwater world.

To Find Out More

Here are some additional resources to help you learn more about tropical fish:

 **Books**

Ancona, George. **The Aquarium Book.** Clarion Books, 1991.

Aronsky, Jim. **Crinkleroot's 25 Fish Every Child Should Know.** Bradbury Press, 1992.

Coupe, Sheena M. **Do Fish Ever Get Thirsty? Questions Answered by Les Kaufman and the Staff of the New England Aquarium.** Franklin Watts, 1991.

Evans, Mark. **Fish.** Dorling Kindersley, 1993.

Ling, Mary. **Amazing Fish.** Knopf, 1991.

Parker, Steve. **Fish.** Knopf, 1990.

☼ Organizations and Online Sites

Acme Pet
http://www.acmepet.com/ fish/

Includes useful information on all kinds of fish.

American Society for the Prevention of Cruelty to Animals (ASPCA)
424 East 92nd Street
New York, NY 10128-6804
(212) 876-7700, ext. 4421
http://www.aspca.org/

This organization is dedicated to the prevention of cruelty to animals. They also provide advice and services for caring for all kinds of animals.

Aquaria Web Services
http://www.cco.caltech. edu/~aquaria/

This Web site includes a list of questions and answers about fish care.

Lycos Mini-Guide to Pet Care
http://www.lycos.com/ lifestyle/miniguide/ petcare.html

A list of online resources relating to pets and pet care.

Petstation
http://petstation.com/ fish.html

An online service for anyone interested in keeping aquarium fish.

Pet Talk
http://www.zmall.com/pet/

An online resource of animal care information.

Important Words

aquarium a glass tank used for keeping fish

chlorine a chemical sometimes added to a water supply to kill germs. Chlorine can be harmful to some fish.

filter a device used to remove impurities from a fish tank's water

gravel a mixture of small rounded stones often used as the bottom layer of an aquarium

miniature something reduced in size

pellets fish food molded into small balls

thrive to flourish or do well

tropical originating in the hot, rainy area of the earth called the tropics

Index

Meet the Author

Elaine Landau worked as a newspaper reporter, children's book editor, and youth services librarian before becoming a full-time writer. She has written more than ninety books for young people.

Ms. Landau lives in Florida with her husband and son.